ALONE
TOGETHER

Edes Powell Gilbert

ISBN: 1-4392-6546-1

ISBN-13: 9781439265468

FOR

TIMOTHY, CHRISTOPHER, AND SARAH

INTRODUCTION

This is a memoir of my life and aspects of my family, from my Brooklyn beginning to my college years. Because I believe that our beginnings hold clues to the people we become, I have written this memoir for my children and grandchildren, who may find some insights into their own lives as they learn about the people of their past. Beyond the personal, this is a period piece of life in downtown New York City during and after World War II. As a girl growing up in those years, the assumptions about the roles of women were largely un-questioned by society as a whole. The traditions of marriage, motherhood, and confining one's life to primarily serving family needs were still very much in force. (Although many women went to work during World War II while the men served overseas, they were expected to go back to their roles at home when the war was over, so that the men would have the jobs.) I was blessed to be in a family where the expectations for graduating from a fine college and successfully engaging in a career were clear, and there was a "tradition" of women working outside the home. I was also expected to marry and have children, which I did soon after completing college. As it happened, I had wanted to be a teacher from the time I was eight years old. Had I wanted to be a CEO of a bank, my life would have been very different. But I settled on teaching and marriage in the knowledge that I was fulfilling my family's expectations. My parents and grandparents were profound influences, each in his or her own way. Their accomplishments and disappointments have become increasingly important to my own ways of being in the world today. This is their story as much, and maybe more, as it is mine. I am grateful for their influence on my life and for the genes they passed on to me and my children. They are all part of my beginning, of the woman that I have become, and of my children and my children's children.

Edes Powell Gilbert
November 2009

CHAPTER 1

EUROPE... OR A BABY?

"Which shall it be?," my recently married parents asked themselves as the Depression was looming. London and Paris? Or a baby? They saved a huge wedding present of a $1,000 bond, not an easy task for two young writers living from paycheck to paycheck in a tiny apartment in Greenwich Village, and dreamed of going to Europe together for a honeymoon, which they postponed because of my journalist father's work at *The New York World Telegram and Sun.* With the economy in a downward spiral, they decided the money would be better spent on starting their family. According to the story my mother told me (which I loved to hear), they turned on the radio looking for some music, and to the yearning melody of "Where or When," they made me. As the years went by and life happened, that story made me feel wanted and important because I knew that my parents had actually decided to have me. I arrived on a cold, gray Good Friday morning in March 1932 at a small lying-in hospital in Brooklyn Heights, having been expected two weeks earlier. My father was on assignment in Washington, so my grandmother and mother welcomed me after an uneventful labor and delivery.

My name, Edes Lawrence, is a combination of family names. (If I had been a boy, my name would have been Anthony because my mother liked the nickname Tony.) Edes is the surname of my mother's family who originated in Sussex, England, and came here early in the eighteenth century. They were champions of personal and religious freedom, frequently at odds with the establishment of the era, and played an active role in the American Revolution. Edes and Gill Printers of Boston printed flyers with news of the war, which were distributed frequently in the Boston area, and were an annoyance to the British leaders who could not stop production of their printed materials. When the British invaded Boston, Benjamin Edes and his colleagues put the printing press on a wooden raft in the dark of night and floated it down the Charles River to Watertown; thereby evading the authorities and not missing a publication deadline. The latter half of my name, Lawrence, came from the Scottish branch of the Powell family who claimed the MacLaren tartan, which was important to me because I had a pleated skirt made from that material. It featured a large brass safety pin, and I loved to wear it when I was in the fifth grade.

My parents, Helen Ann Ranney Powell and Talcott Williams Powell, were in some ways typical of a certain group of aspiring writers and artists who migrated to Greenwich Village in downtown New York City during the twenties. They were transplants from other places and lives, full of big dreams and charm as well as attractive and sophisticated, or so they appear in the few pictures that I have. My mother grew up in Newark, Ohio, raised by formidable Aunt Anna Bradshaw Herzog and affable Uncle Jack Herzog, who had no children of their own. Her mother, Susan Bradshaw Ranney, went overseas as a nurse during and after World War I. She was trained to work with the victims of shell shock and was given an extended term of service in the army. She was away for eight or nine years, which had a profound effect on her relationship with my mother. It seemed to me, during my childhood and into my teen years, that the two women were never close, although they were in touch by letter regularly. My grandmother, whom I called "Mummy's Mummy," later abbreviated to "MM" to distinguish her from my other grandmother, came to visit occasionally from Toledo, Ohio, where she lived with an elderly cousin, Ethel Hamilton. One year she made a skirt with small, dense blue and green flowers for an old dressing table that was in my room. I kept it for many years and thought it was beautiful. She regaled me with stories about her life, one of which told of her love of horseback riding in the wilds of Southern California where she and her husband, William St. John Ranney, had settled in the early 1900s. My mother was born there in 1906, followed by a brother who died in infancy. My grandmother told me she rode in the first Rose Parade in Pasadena and gave vivid descriptions of the pink rose petals on the road and the horses, many of which were work horses from the local farms. Most of the time she rode in the hills with a group of her friends while her husband worked in the local bank. She told me more than once that "Bill was the most attractive man I ever knew," and she never remarried after she left him in 1912, when he went to prison for embezzling funds from the bank. She and my mother boarded a train east to Newark, Ohio, to start a new life. I remember my mother receiving a red velvet Christmas card from Texas one year from her father, who was in prison for life. Apparently he could not stop taking money from others. She spoke of him in terse terms only a few times and said nothing when she opened the card. It went on the pile of cards on the hall table with no comment.

In her Newark High School yearbook, my mother looked beautiful and wistful. She was fair-skinned with reddish-brown hair, which she wore all her life in a kind of French twist, and had blue eyes that were clear and inscrutable. Her bearing was confident and erect. She apparently did well in school and, at my grandmother's insistence, applied to and was accepted at Vassar College. She was eager to leave Newark and the very stringent household of Aunt Anna and Uncle Jack; they took good care of her, but their lives were deeply entangled with the Christian Science Church for which Aunt Anna was a Reader. More importantly, she missed her mother. After serving in the army, my grandmother became head nurse at Michael Reese Hospital in Toledo, Ohio, earning enough money to support her daughter and herself, but not enough to have her daughter live with her; not an easy decision, I am sure, and one which left my mother with a lifelong resentment. I came across her journal years ago, and her hurt and rage at her mother was described over and over, as well as her dislike of the life she led with her aunt and uncle. Her years at college were shrouded in mystery for me, as she did not want to talk much about them, which was odd because she was ready to talk with me about every other imaginable subject, an attribute my friends envied and I treasured. I sent for her transcript several years ago and found that she had been a mediocre student and, for whatever reason, had taken five years to complete her degree in English. She was delighted when I chose to attend Vassar, and I heard snippets about her time there; but they were mainly about climbing in and out of dormitory windows when she got back to campus after curfew, and the many "boys" she went out with in New York to various speakeasies and loft apartments. As far as I know, she made no lifelong friends in college, and I do not remember meeting anyone who knew her during those years.

She did tell me about her life after college (she graduated in 1927), when she went to work at Macy's in their advertising and copywriting departments. There she met Isobel Strong who became one of her closest friends and my godmother. The two bobbed their hair, bound their breasts, and led a very "twenties" life, working hard by day and playing hard by night. They shared many tales of making and drinking bathtub gin, getting abortions in Harlem when the birth control of the time (pessaries) failed or was ignored, and living three and four "girls" to an apartment on Perry or Christopher Streets. Another friend of hers was rumored to be one of Tom Wolfe's mistresses. In any case, they were a group of smart, lively, hardworking, and hard-playing young women who kept in touch through the ensuing years.

My father, named for the dean of journalism at Columbia University, Talcott Williams, was a tall man with dark hair and eyes. He was dynamic, talented, and gregarious, and especially enjoyed the company of women, who found him sexy and a bit dangerous. I remember him in unrelated vignettes with the common thread of me feeling beloved and safe when

I was with him. We laughed together over nothing in particular. When he played the accordion and sang "Blow the Man Down" I was mesmerized. I remember going with him in a rowboat on Long Island Sound and the tide went out, leaving us unable to get close enough to the dock to disembark. He lifted me up over the smelly mud, his hands firm and reassuring on my rib cage. My mother reached out and grabbed me with a huge hug. I have no idea how he got onto dry land himself.

Brilliant and complicated, Talcott was the son of an Episcopal minister, Lyman Pierson Powell, who was himself a writer of a number of books; the most well-known of which was a biography, *Mary Baker Eddy*. He also wrote a weekly column in *The Christian Science Monitor*. My two granddaughters and I visited the Mother Church of Christian Science in Boston several years ago and saw copies of the book, which was still in print. He was president of Hobart College in Geneva, New York, from 1913 to 1918 and served as minister at St. Margaret's Church in the Bronx and St. John's Church in Northampton, Massachusetts, before and after that appointment. He lectured in the United States and abroad on subjects related to peace and issues of social equity. Granddaddy and I spent many afternoons together whenever I visited my grandparents, talking and listening to him tell stories about his life. Sometimes he allowed me to polish his silver traveling communion set, which he used for home visits when parishioners were unable to attend St. Peter's Church in Mountain Lakes, New Jersey, where he was minister for ten years. Although Granddaddy was not tall, he had great presence. His hair was snowy white, carefully brushed back on his head, his eyes were very blue, always kind and often sparkly, and he wore rimless glasses on a black ribbon around his neck. I often wondered how they held their perch on his nose when he wore them, but I never saw them slip off. A disciplined man, he wrote from 5:00 a.m. to 8:00 a.m., six days a week; after which he tossed down a raw egg for breakfast and dressed in his white shirt and dark suit with a jaunty straw boater in the summer, preparatory to his daily walk. Every Sunday during my summers with them, my grandmother took me to church, where we always sat in the front row. From there, I watched my grandfather in his black cassock and white surplice conduct the service and preach high up in the pulpit. I often thought about this person who looked and sounded like God and, yet, was also the "Granddaddy" with whom I had happy times sitting on his lap with my dolls at the end of many hot summer afternoons discussing the day's happenings. When I later was instructed in Sunday School about a "loving God" I understood. After church we would stand and greet everyone, then we walked home to Sunday dinner and a quiet afternoon. I was not allowed to play outside until evening, out of respect for the Sabbath; I was permitted to read or play quietly with my paper dolls.

Talcott's mother, Gertrude Wilson Powell, had grown up in the Philadelphia area and was a graduate of Wellesley College. She became a history teacher at the Emma Willard School in Troy, New York, where she and Lyman met and married in 1899. She was an austere woman with rimless glasses and gray hair with yellow streaks, which she wore pulled back tight in a bun at the nape of her neck. Her feet were firmly placed and laced into sensible black shoes with a low heel, and her stockings, which she wore on the hottest of summer days, were made of beige cotton lisle. Her dresses all seemed the same to me, with buttons up the front of a floral pattern cotton and a narrow belt that buckled in the front and rubbed my cheek when I hugged her. She wore no jewelry except for her wedding ring. Her austerity was tempered by a deep, loving devotion to me, and I felt her care for and about me. She made many of my clothes during the time when I was very young. Her sewing machine with the metal treadle that looked like a fancy filigree was on the third floor. The room was hot and had no furnishings except the chair where she sat as she worked on my fall wardrobe each summer. She and I chose the materials and the patterns for my dresses at the Dry Goods Store in Boonton, New Jersey, and I learned to stand very still while she measured and pinned. I remember one of my favorite dresses, which was dark blue with a white collar, a sash in the back, and tiny pink and white flowers. I can imagine that making girls' clothes after two sons and no other granddaughter must have given her great pleasure, and I was happy to have new dresses for school.

My father was one of two brothers born eight years apart. He was as strong and healthy as his brother was weak and sickly. He was always a highly energetic, articulate person who, according to his mother, could "charm the birds off the trees." He had many friends and was, I gather, something of a rebel in the straitlaced home that Gertrude ran with a steady iron hand. Liquor was forbidden, and when my parents visited, they packed flasks that they opened and sipped from in the guest room. Also, he smoked at an early age, which was another anathema to my grandmother. It was a habit he and my mother shared, and when they visited his parents, they disposed of their butts in a large ugly green jar with two lizards crawling up it, whose mouths were open to receive the forbidden Chesterfield stubs. I knew the jar well, and when I visited in subsequent years, I spent some time and effort trying to peer inside and see if any of my father's smoked cigarettes might still be in there. He attended several schools, public and private, leaving his college career at Wesleyan University unfinished in favor of going to work as a reporter for the newspaper in Middletown, New York. When he and my mother met at a speakeasy in Harlem in 1929, he was in the midst of divorcing his first wife, Ysabel Loney, with whom he had a son, David Talcott, my half-brother. David was seven years older than me and looked a lot like our father. I was fascinated by him, although I did not see him as often as I would have liked, as he lived with his mother and stepfather in Philadelphia. We were connected in a profound way, and when he was drafted into the army out of his freshman year at Harvard, where he was a pre-med student, we wrote letters to each other on the tiny pale blue V-Mail, which was the special mail service for people in the armed services during World War II. By then, at thirteen, I had dreams for the future and questions about our father, which were subjects we wrote to each other about. He described a Belgian family that had become his friends and a kind of loving extended family. He was killed in 1945 and is buried in Belgium, where the family took care of his grave for years. His death made me angry and resentful as well as deeply sad and lonely. When we received the news that he was missing in action in late October, I put it out of my mind and refused to think about his being killed.

When his death was confirmed late in November, I cried for hours and off and on for days. It seems to me now that I cried for my father as well as my brother, and even after all these years, I have a lump in my throat as I write these words.

CHAPTER II

NEWSPAPER NOMADS

I have no idea where we lived immediately after I was born; I assume somewhere in Brooklyn or Manhattan. However, by the time I was around two, my father was hired by the *Indianapolis Tribune* to write a series exposing the entrenched political machine that was governing Indianapolis, Indiana, at that time. With Hazel, my caretaker and the family sustainer, we boarded an overnight train for the Midwest and moved into an apartment in a red brick building with a small grassy courtyard in downtown Indianapolis. It was the first of several moves we would make following my father on assignment. My mother told me the story about the time we spent there, which I did not fully understand until years later when I read an article about my father being a champion of issues of equity and justice. She and I had been "smuggled" out of the city at midnight into Kentucky because our lives had been threatened by the local political machine in reaction to a series he had written investigating corruption within the local government. It was a romantic and sinister tale that became part of the family lore.

After our dramatic departure from Indiana, we came back to the East Coast where my father went back to work for the *World Telegram and Sun,* and we lived, for a short time, in a small white house with tall trees and a yard in Stamford, Connecticut. Soon, he was sent on a new assignment to research the myths surrounding the Fountain of Youth, alleged to be somewhere on an island in the Caribbean. We packed up and prepared to move to San Juan, Puerto Rico, in the fall of 1936. This time Hazel did not join us. It was the first of my experiences on a freighter that was designed to carry cargo, but had four or five small cabins in the stern with no other amenities beyond shared bathrooms and toilets. It was cold on the ocean, and I was bundled up in a navy blue coat, leggings, and a beret. My mother wore a brown tweed coat, which was rough and scratchy to my touch, and of course a hat and gloves, as they were expected accessories at all times in the thirties and, in this case, much needed. On deck, there was a row of brown wooden deck chairs where Mother spent her days reading, while I sported a harness with a leash that was hooked over the back of her deck chair. This arrangement was essential, as the railings on the ship were high and I could have slipped under easily with one big wave rolling the ship even slightly. The smell of the salt water and the hypnotic rising and falling of the swells became my familiar world on this journey, which took about ten days because the ship made several stops to unload and take on big, bulging canvas bags of goods, odd pieces of furniture, and a few people who faded into the life onboard our floating world.

My trusty companion on this trip was Mousie, my imaginary playmate. He was soft, gray, compliant, and had "a pink ribbon on his ear." Obligingly, he sat on the railing and reported back to me, at the end of my leash, all he was seeing in ports and on the water. He joined us for dinner in the airless, small dining room where we had our meals. A place, complete with a chair and a pillow, was always set for him by the steward, who joined my mother in acknowledging the importance of Mousie. He and I dined each evening on a bowl of spinach with a poached egg on top, as the other culinary offerings were judged to be inappropriate for a child—and her mouse. I have vivid memories of those cracked white bowls with blobs of dark green spinach and the egg, trembling on top, waiting for me to spear it with my fork. (I always took care to pierce Mousie's egg as well, although he did not care for the menu.) Sailing on a freighter was an adventure Mother and I both enjoyed, as we sailed toward the unknown San Juan, Puerto Rico, where my father was working and had found us a place to live.

Our apartment was on the ground floor of a building that featured terra-cotta tiled floors, many windows, and dazzling white walls in every room. There were also cockroaches, large and small, which shared the space with us, uninvited and ubiquitous. A person who became very important to me during our months there was Ramon, the caretaker of the building, a thin, wiry man of indeterminate age with a big smile. He wore a brimmed cloth hat and work pants rolled up to his knees, held up with a rope around his narrow waist. Ramon spoke no English and I may have imitated a few words of Spanish, but we could not talk together easily; however, this did not stop us from communicating. He arrived shortly after breakfast each day, with a gray string mop and a bucket of water, to begin the daily ritual of floor washing. I gathered up my doll to follow him and listen as he swished the mop and talked to me in low tones in Spanish. Later in the afternoon, Mother and I would walk to the sweeping expanse of white beach near the apartment building, I with a small pail and a shovel and she with a towel and a book. Except for the itchiness of the navy blue wool bathing suit I wore, the long afternoons of playing in the sand and water were a happy ritual.

At some point, we were joined by an American boy about my age named Jimmy, with blond hair that stuck up in points all over is head. His main contribution to our months in Puerto Rico was to pass on a raging case of measles to me. I spent days in a dark room in a screened-in crib that was really a cage with the top down so that the various bugs would not get to me. I lay there watching cockroaches parading across the mesh over my head and wishing I were at the beach. Ramon visited me often during his daily rounds and swatted the bugs with vigor if not with many successful results. Soon after my recovery, my parents and I celebrated Christmas with a scrawny hybrid tree that I found unsatisfactory and a couple of gifts for each of us. This was also an occasion for my father to play the accordion, which he did imperfectly but with gusto. His rollicking version of "Adeste Fideles" sounded loud and we all sang.

By spring, the three of us were back on a freighter, chugging up the East Coast to New York City. After months of research, the conclusion was that there was no Fountain of Youth, and the newspaper wanted my father back in the New York office. He was already starting his work on World War I veterans' benefits, which he considered to be woefully inadequate, and the *Telegram-Sun* was very interested in the project. It subsequently ran this as a series, which my father later turned into a book, *Tattered Banners*, winning a Pulitzer for himself and the paper. We moved into a two-story yellow clapboard house in Old Greenwich, Connecticut, with a front porch, a fireplace in the living room, and many windows in the bedrooms that looked out onto the Long Island Sound. My parents had a number of friends in the area as well as in New York, and the house was full of people on the weekends. I also got my first dog, a collie named Pat. Hazel rejoined our lives with her unprepossessing, but very affable, husband, Leroy, who came on many weekends. He did occasional chores, but mainly sat on a faded blue wooden chair in the kitchen, which he tilted back, and told a steady stream of stories about nothing in particular, as far as I could tell. He always seemed to be watching Hazel who was a tireless worker and took care of our domestic life in all its details, since my mother had no interest in or patience for housework. She grew to like cooking later in her life, but it was an acquired, not an innate, skill. One of her great household moments was her realization one morning that there was a button to be sewed on one of her skirts, without which the skirt would fall off. Finding a needle and thread was the first step and took some time and effort. Then, in preparation for the ordeal ahead, she poured and drank a shot glass of bourbon. The actual sewing took five minutes at the most. The whole episode took over half an hour, and even as a young child I thought it was funny. Drinking in the morning was not part of our family routine, but neither was sewing!

My fifth birthday in the yellow house in Stamford was not a happy time. My father had been ill for several days and was admitted to the hospital the day before the party that had been planned for some time. He was diagnosed with acute appendicitis, which became a ruptured appendix and then peritonitis set in. His doctor had made the erroneous diagnosis of "indigestion," and by the time the correct diagnosis was made, it was too late. On the day he left for the hospital, I was in their bedroom with them as he put on his tie and struggled into a dark blue jacket, doubled over in pain. I was "dusting" my mother's bureau and my parents were talking together in low tones. Mother looked different, pale and with no lovely smile. As we left the room, my mother carried a small suitcase. My father took my hand as we went down the stairs together and out onto the porch. Mother had driven our car to the end of the cement walk that sparkled in the spring sun as it went in a straight line from the porch to the street. My father walked slowly down the steps and onto the walk, turning slightly to blow me a kiss. He stepped into the car, waved again, and was gone, out of my life forever.

Hazel and Leroy presided over my birthday party that year. My friend and playmate, Joel, was there as was Susan, daughter of Mother's friend Isobel from her years at Macy's and still my dearest friend. There were a couple of other children whose faces and names have long since vanished into the mists of the long-ago past. Hazel adored my father and was crying as she put the cake on the table for me to blow out the candles. No one had told me that my father was ill, and my parents wanted me to have my celebration as planned. Hazel wept silently throughout party, and when the time came to clear the table, Leroy "helped" by walking behind her, propping her up with his hands on her waist while she carried the dishes.

My father, just thirty-seven years old, died the next day. Suddenly, the house was full of people and my mother was wearing black. I was alternately fussed over and ignored while funeral arrangements and plans for the immediate future were being made by Mother and her friends, who were attentive and thoughtful to our needs in the midst of a profoundly sad time. I did not attend the funeral, which was held in New York City. His father, my grandfather, Lyman Powell, the Episcopal minister, led the service. It was an occasion that many of those who attended could not even mention in the ensuing years without weeping.

The next day, my mother and I boarded the train for New Orleans, where we got on another cargo ship and sailed through the Panama Canal to my grandmother, Mummy's Mummy as I called her, who was waiting for us in San Diego. A high point of the trip was watching the Panamanians come alongside our ship in canoes and rafts to sell their grapefruits and carved wooden knickknacks. The sing-song cadence of the Spanish was intriguing to me. It made me remember happier times in Puerto Rico with Ramon and our "conversations."

We settled into a peaceful, sunny life in my grandmother's cottage, with its flagstone patio shaded by trees and adorned with large clay pots of geraniums as well as comfortable wicker chairs; one of which was large enough for me to sit on her lap while she read stories to me. I have no memories of my mother during the ensuing four months, but many of my grandmother who taught me to knit and took me to the San

Diego Zoo, where the statues of storybook characters stood along the paths between the animal exhibits. Everyday I was in charge of watering the geraniums, a task that I enjoy to this day as I water flowers on my own patio. Later in her life, my mother was engulfed by depression, and this time may have been such an episode, a result of losing the husband she adored at the age of thirty-one. She once told me, years later, that when my father died she grew up, and she mused about whether she would have grown up if he had lived.

CHAPTER III

MOTHER AND ME

After several months of sunny Southern California and being cared for by my grandmother, Mother and I boarded the train for the five day cross-country trip to New York City. She had resolved to start a new life and had a circle of friends who encouraged her to return to the City where she had been happy in years past. We moved into a tiny garden apartment on West 12th Street, and I acquired a large, ornery yellow cat named Fluffy. I started school at a one-room school on 8th Street and Fifth Avenue called Lad and Lassie. Hazel, who had cared for me until we went to California and who had adored my father, came back into our lives and made it possible for my mother to return to work. She lived in Brooklyn with Leroy and his daughter, Evelyn, who had arrived unexpectedly from Hazel's point of view, as she was the result of Leroy's philandering. Evelyn and I played together whenever we were not in school; she was two or three years younger than me and allowed me to flex my teaching and supervisory muscles at an early age. I was sure that I taught Evelyn to read, although as I grew older, I had to grudgingly give her teachers some of the credit. That feeling of excitement at the moment when teaching becomes learning stayed with me throughout my years as an elementary school teacher. Hazel worked for my mother for twelve dollars a week, which even then was a low wage for five to six days of ten to twelve hours a day, but she once told me that she wanted more than anything to be a part of our lives. She introduced me to the Brooklyn Dodgers and the *Daily News*, both essentials for a New Yorker to appreciate.

Lad and Lassie probably would not have survived the layers of regulations of today. It was a school of twenty or so students, grades K–5. The kindergarten had one room and the other five grades were all together in another, and we were taught by Mrs. Willoner. There was one bathroom with yellow tiles. Mme. De Boutillier was the proprietress and had her apartment in the back, where she prepared (among other things) gallons of lentil soup redolent with garlic. Occasionally, we were offered some of her culinary creations, and I have always believed that my lifelong fondness for garlic began with them. The classes were very fluid, in that if Mrs. Willoner thought a first grader was ready to read with the second grade then she organized us that way. I was a reader at five, so I had all sorts of classes with second and third graders, while in arithmetic and penmanship I was less proficient and stayed on grade level. I do not remember feeling any particular emotion about my placement either way, and I have a great professional regard as well as a personal fondness for Mrs. Willoner, who must have been a most accomplished teacher. I do recall being fascinated when she was pregnant and even more delighted when she brought the infant to school and nursed her. Several years ago, I met the president of Bowdoin College at that time, Bob

Edwards, who remembered me when I was a fifth grader and he was in the third grade. We agreed that we had been given an extraordinary elementary school experience and found it even more remarkable that the two of us had attended a one-room school on 8ᵗʰ Street in New York City at the same time. Lad and Lassie went out of business sometime during World War II, after I had been enrolled at Friends Seminary midway through the fifth grade. It seems that Mme. DeBoutillier lost her ability to make good decisions for the students in her care, and when it was essential for us to practice evacuating our building in the required air-raid drills, she led us all to a basement room full of steam pipes in a nearby building. My mother judged this to be imprudent and decided to cast our lot with the Quakers, who gave me a generous scholarship to attend Friends Seminary.

My first day there remains a vivid memory. I was greeted at the front door by Mary Burdell, a dark-eyed girl with wavy dark hair, who I thought was beautiful. She was wearing a pink linen-type suit with a white ruffled blouse that completed a picture I found amazing and a bit exotic. She led me up the stairs to the fifth grade classroom where the bespectacled Miss Mercer sat behind her desk reading *The Oregon Trail* aloud, a practice that became a favorite part of my new school. Following her reading aloud, Miss Mercer, who was not tall and quite round, went to the blackboard. In measured, precise handwriting she wrote out the first eleven verses of Paul's First Letter to the Corinthians, chapter 13, which famously begins, "Though I speak in the tongues of men and of angels…" After reading it together, we were then given the assignment to memorize it for the next day. I still remember much of that

Bible passage. Moving from room to room for our classes and listening to the squeaking sound of the boys' corduroy knickers were daily features of the fifth grade that became routine very quickly. The required air-raid drills involved sitting on the floor in the inside hallways of a sturdy apartment building across the street, with our knees drawn up and our faces pressed against them and our arms hugging our legs. It seems quaint in retrospect, but New York took wartime precautions very seriously, from blackout curtains in every apartment to civilian air patrols staffed by volunteers in hard hats on the rooftops of tall buildings and regular drills day and night. There was a strong sense of what we now call "bonding" among all New Yorkers, whatever their background or social status. Patriotism was fierce and unquestioned.

Hazel picked me up from school almost every day at one o'clock, and when the weather was good, we went to Washington Square. I learned to roller-skate (but never very well), roll a hoop without colliding with too many people, play hopscotch, and most of all, jump rope, especially Double Dutch with one or two other playmates. From my earliest years, Mother and Hazel cautioned me against going into the sandbox, as they had seen too many dogs and neighborhood cats using it as a latrine. I, of course, considered that a deprivation, but abided by the rule nonetheless. In the late afternoon, we would walk home to 12th Street, where I did homework, had my bath and supper, and waited for my mother to come home. Hazel would put on her black hat, with a small gray feather adorning it, and her black coat, hug me, and leave. Mother and I would sit together in the big stuffed chair in the living room with a lamp, and she read to me. It was the time of day that I loved more than anything else in our life together. She read me L. Frank Baum's *OZ* books, Rudyard Kipling's *Just So Stories, The Jungle Book,* and *The Second Jungle Book, The Secret Garden,* and I am sure many others. She made me into a voracious reader, a habit that has brought me sustenance, solace, entertainment, and learning over the years, and a gift I have tried to pass on to my own children and grandchildren.

On occasional weekends, she and I would go to a movie, which was a big and sometimes scary happening. I begged to leave during *Fantasia* when the dinosaurs roamed the screen and Snow White's sinister stepmother terrified me. We actually left the theatre only that one time, but I learned to cover my eyes when it got spooky, a practice I have continued all my life. Other times, we went to the Metropolitan Museum to see the Egyptian exhibit with the mummy of a Pharaoh, scrawny and wrapped in grayish bindings, and for me to play in a replica of a stone house from some long-ago culture. Climbing the big rocks in Central Park was another favorite of mine. Mother would wait patiently for me to get to the top and proclaim my dominion over all I surveyed, and then we would get on the bus and go back to 12th Street. If it happened to be a lucky day, we would ride on the top of an open-air Fifth Avenue bus, which was an experience that never lost its charm for me. Very occasionally, she took me to Best and Company, where I acquired winter coats, usually blue double-breasted tweed with a velveteen collar, and leggings with leather legs and a dark blue wool upper section that, at times, chafed my thighs until they bled. The remedy was Hinds lotion, which had such a sting to it that I would dance around yelping. Other less affecting purchases were shoes—saddle shoes for school and Mary Janes for "party" shoes—and muslin under-pants with eyelet trim. I was dressed well, but did not have many clothes by today's standards. I never had more than one coat, two pairs of shoes, a cardigan, two or three "everyday" dresses, a skirt and a blouse, and one "party" dress.

The Christmas following my father's death, my mother and I went to my grandparents' home in Mountain Lakes. It was the only time I ever had Christmas with them. I felt snug and happy in my usual bedroom adjacent to my grand-mother's room, which was across the broad hallway from my grandfather's room. I woke up in the middle of the night to hear the sound of reindeer on the roof, and when I reported this the next morning, the grown-ups all smiled. I did not believe in Santa Claus, nor did I disbelieve. He was a figure in a poem I loved, *The Night Before Christmas.* But I did believe in reindeer on the roof! Going downstairs to the beautiful tree that had magically appeared overnight, I saw my heart's desire—a pink wicker baby doll carriage with a Didey Doll, complete with a change of clothes and a pink and white blan-ket. No present has ever meant so much to me, and I imagine now that my happiness must have been a moment of joy for my grieving mother and grandparents.

My mother and I lived peacefully in our tiny apartment. She slept late on weekends, and I tiptoed around with Fluffy and my dolls and books. Hazel came and went, and between the two women I was well cared for. I can remember only one punishment during those years, when one evening at supper I flushed the lima beans, which I loathed, down the toilet. Why I thought this would go unnoticed in our small space, I cannot imagine. My mother summarily turned me facedown across her lap and whacked my bottom a couple of times with her hairbrush, explaining clearly that I was never, ever to waste food. Whether I liked it or not, I was lucky to have it, and I was to eat it without comment. I was mortified and crushed, having never been spanked. I was also angry because I *hated* lima beans, so why did I have to eat them anyway?

As a freelance writer, Mother wrote for several magazines, but one I remember, that published some of her work was called *YOU.* She wrote nonfiction articles; one I have read was about traveling with a small child and was based on our adventures following my father on his various assignments. However, writing was not a dependable source of income, and although she had a modest amount each month from a $10,000 life insurance policy that my father had taken out when I was born, she needed to work. She found a position as a secretary/companion/driver to Cornelia Plumb, a lovely and dignified woman who had been crippled by arthritis at a very young age and needed assistance to lead the full life that she chose. During the summer months when I was not with my paternal grandparents, where I spent most of my vacations during those years, Mrs. Plumb would invite me to join her and my mother at a beach club on Long Island. I had never seen a cabana, and the gaily striped canvas structures were fascinating to me. Having lunch magically appear on trays with accompanying tables was another marvel. I spent hours in the water and building sand castles. Although I played by myself during those days—she had no children, nor were any others invited—I was encouraged by Mrs. Plumb to converse, and she treated me with respect and fondness. Those outings were the first bit of glamour that I experienced during my childhood years. Later on, when I married, Mrs. Plumb sent us salad plates from Tiffany's as a wedding gift, and so the aura of glamour continued.

Summer vacations during these years (when I was five to nine years old) were spent with Grandmother and Granddaddy in their big stucco house on Hanover Road in Mountain Lakes. Each June, Mother would take me to Penn Station, where she put me on the Lackawanna Railroad train to Boonton, New Jersey. I had a tag pinned to my dress with my name and destination, as well as a return address. My grandparents would be waiting at the station and we would board the bus to Mountain Lakes. Life was peaceful and routine there. My room featured a white iron bed with a pale green seersucker counterpane. It faced the front of the house where a huge oak tree spread its branches, shading the front lawn and the "porte cochere" that covered the driveway in front of the heavy oak door, which led to a dark paneled hallway. The living room was on the right and the dining room on the left, a room that was furnished with a dark, shiny sideboard and table with six high backed chairs with unyielding seats. Three windows opened onto the veranda that ran the length of the house. White lace curtains and crocheted table covers festooned the sideboard and table. There was one light in the ceiling with a frosted glass cover over it. My grandparents sat at either end of the oval table, and I sat between my grandparents, where I could see out to the porch with the comfortable wicker and canvas furniture. My grandparents and I spent many summer afternoons reading and talking in the relative coolness of that porch.

One summer, my Uncle Francis (my father's brother) built me a playhouse at the end of the backyard. I spent many happy hours there with my dolls and my friend, Virginia Lamb, who lived across the street and with whom I played almost every day. Like me, she had braids and wore cotton dresses and open leather sandal-type shoes with white socks. Unlike me, she had large brown eyes and dark brown hair. We were both imaginative and loved playing "pretend." No one else seemed to notice this until the day I instructed her in how to nurse a baby, which I had seen Mrs. Willoner do at school and my mother had endorsed as a natural and normal process. My grandmother was horrified; she took me into the kitchen, where she lectured me on "nice" girl behavior, and forced me to stand in the corner facing the wall for what seemed like hours. I must have written my mother about this episode or told her when I got home in the fall. In any case, she called my grandmother—which was an event in itself, as phones were seldom used except in emergencies. From what I learned later, she was outraged at that treatment of me and at the message about nursing, which she considered to be wrong in the extreme.

All I knew at the time was that the following summer I did not visit my grandparents, and instead went to a small farm/camp in Hubbardston, Massachusetts, run by the Peabodys. There were fourteen of us, boys and girls ranging in age from nine to fourteen or so. I spent three or four happy summers there, learning to swim in a pond that had leeches, which were very persuasive in motivating me to swim, so I could get away from shore where they lurked. Other favored activities included going on "snipe hunts" after dark in the woods, which were deliciously scary, and playing endless, spirited games of Tag, Capture the Flag, and Kick the Can.

Each week, on Saturday evening, we went into the village of Hubbardston to attend the band concert with square dancing afterward. Milling around the town common with ice cream cones and Hershey bars while listening to the lively music, played with more enthusiasm than talent, was a high point each week. On rainy days, we took over the living room of the gray Cape Cod house that was the Peabody's home and ours for the summer, making huge tents from our sheets and blankets in which we sat and played Chinese Checkers and Gin Rummy. Ruth and Nancy Peabody, twin daughters of Dean and Mrs. Peabody (he was a dean at MIT, and I never knew their first names), were our counselors. I developed my first crush, which I maintained for two years, on Ruth, who I fancied took a special interest in me.

During those childhood years, when my mother was leading a full social life as well as being a working mother, we spent many weekends with her good friend from her Macy's days, Isobel Strong Hunter. She was my godmother, and a more dynamic, dramatic, and charismatic woman is hard to imagine. The first time I saw *Auntie Mame* I thought it must have been based on Isobel and her sometimes flamboyant but always elegant style. She had glossy black hair, snapping dark eyes, and a mouth that produced improbably broad smiles and was always adorned with bright red lipstick. Her wardrobe was colorful and dramatic, with large clanking jewelry. Her laugh was loud but not displeasing, and her ability to listen carefully before uttering a sharp and amusing remark made her someone I admired inordinately. She had married soon after my mother and father, and had a daughter, Susan, who became and still is my dearest friend. Isobel then fell in love with a handsome advertising executive, John Fistere, who had joined the Office of Secret Service during World War II, and divorced her husband.

While John was away she lived near Gramercy Park, with weekends spent at a small white Cape Cod-style house in Cos Cob, Connecticut. Weekend house parties there were exciting and disturbing. The usual activities, which started on Friday night, involved an indeterminate number of men and women, some married and some not, who worked in the worlds of advertising and entertainment for the most part. The cocktail hour started early, dinner arrived later in the evening, and the party continued until well past midnight, and in some cases, until dawn. When Susan and I were included, we were put to bed around six or so in a large linen cupboard, I on the higher shelf and she below, a la bunk beds, because she was younger and quite frail, having had mastoid problems with her ears for several years. We spent hours pushing the doors of the cupboard open enough to see what was going on, but not enough so we would be discovered, although I doubt anyone was noticing the cupboard or its doors. Eventually we fell asleep, and when we woke, there were people asleep on the floor and on the couches; some clothed and some not, some entwined and some not. There was a certain Bacchanalian quality about the scene, but Susan and I took it for granted and went to the tiny kitchen, which was usually awash in dirty dishes and smelled of stale rye whiskey and old cigarettes, where we found some breakfast—often leftovers from dinner. One of our favorites was key lime pie, which Isobel made with condensed milk and was rich beyond imagining. The adults generally slept late and rose cautiously around noon with hangovers that must have been colossal. We were the objects of some undivided attention for a brief time, and "helped" in the kitchen with preparations for dinner after breakfast/lunches had been eaten informally, to say the least. We were happy to be needed if only temporarily and sometimes would be invited to ride to town on a round of errands. I remember that once someone had a car with a rumble seat, and we sat in it feeling very grown-up with the wind in our hair as we rode down Cognewaugh Road.

On the weekends, when we were not included in the house party or any other activity, Susan and I alternated between staying at her apartment or mine. At hers, we were allowed to read comic books, an activity forbidden by my mother, and to chew gum, also forbidden to me. She had a caretaker, Alberta, who looked after us the way Hazel did when we were at my apartment. At mine, we enjoyed exploring Washington Square, going up to the roof of the building and peering over the side, and, one of our favorites, lying on my bed and sticking our bare feet out the window and wiggling our toes, rain or shine. Looking back at this time, I know both our mothers looked out for us and more or less saw that we were safe and fed, but as single working women in their early thirties, they lived full lives of which we, their daughters, were an important but not central part. The style of parenting at that time was generally more remote than is the custom today. Spending time with children beyond reading to them, taking them on an occasional outing to the park or a museum, and seeing that they did their homework was simply not part of family life in New York City at that time. My friends and I had our lives and our parents had theirs. Occasionally they intersected, but we, as children, were never to disturb the grown-ups, nor did we expect to have to spend much time with them. We were expected to have good manners, which included standing up whenever an adult came into the room, saying "excuse me" if we had any questions during an adult conversation, waiting to eat until everyone was served, saying "please" and "thank you," and generally being seen but not heard. We learned early on not to complain when we had a cold or some other childhood malady and were not encouraged to take such episodes very seriously. It was clear that a sick child was an inconvenience, unless the child became very ill, at which point doctors paid house calls, mothers rallied around, and caretakers worked overtime. Once it was thought that I had appendicitis, which was most alarming to my mother due to my father's death, and I remember feeling astonished at how she hovered and fussed over me when my stomach was hurting, and the doctor was examining me. I found it quite comforting, and spent time later trying to figure out how to get her to cosset me when I did not have a stomachache.

I spent a great deal of time alone in those years. There was usually an adult nearby, but I was left to my own devices. I created imaginary worlds with my dolls and various invented characters. Beyond the worlds I created, I read avidly and broadly. I was never told not to read any book or magazine, so consequently, I lived on a varied diet of literature ranging from *Little Women* to *The Forsyte Saga* to *The New York Post*, with many other articles and books in between. Newspapers and magazines were always on the coffee table, and my mother had books by her bed as well as tucked in shelves and under tables throughout the apartment.

After three or four years of life together on West 12th Street, a classmate of my father's at Wesleyan called my mother after he had seen Talcott Powell's name in the phone book. My mother kept her number listed under his name, feeling that it was safer than being listed as a single woman. Fred Anderson was an admirer of my father and wanted to meet his widow. He came to our tiny apartment one evening, when I was reading the *Daily News* on the floor. As they sat on the couch and talked, I came across a story in the newspaper about a rape and asked my mother what that meant. Long afterward, Fred told me it was at that moment that he became intrigued by and admiring of my mother because of the forthright and respectful way she answered my question. They were married in August 1943 after several years of courtship.

CHAPTER IV

FAMILY AND FARM

Today it is called a "blended family;" that is, when two people marry and each have children from previous marriages. My stepfather, Fred Anderson, had two sons who were seven and eight years older than me. For reasons that were never clear to me, they lived in a boarding house in Doylestown, Pennsylvania, where they went to high school. Their mother, Ann, had died at age twenty-five or twenty-six of stomach cancer, and Fred had gone into a deep depression, neglecting the boys, who spent time with their grandparents and various caretakers for a couple of years. When he emerged from that dark time, he married a woman, Gerry, who had a son she doted on. The two brothers were consigned to the third floor in minimum quarters, while her son lived in a large bedroom on the second floor next to the master bedroom. The story had a vaguely Cinderella aura about it, but whatever the stark truth was, the effects of those years on the two boys were devastating; they emerged into young manhood damaged by years of trauma of one kind or another. I could not imagine why their father sent them away at ages fourteen and fifteen to a boarding house in Doylestown where they attended high school. After graduation, the younger one, Roger, earned his engineering degree from Rensselaer Polytechnic Institute, and the older brother, Freddy, went into the army.

Freddy was a person tormented by self-doubts and the possibility that he was gay, which was a subject that drove my stepfather into a paroxysm of rage whenever it was mentioned in any context. Fred's language was peppered with the phrase "goddamn faggots" and loud statements about not having "pansies" in his house. My mother and I worried about Freddy, who was not around very much (understandably!), but when he was home, he was anxious and pacing. He eventually was diagnosed as manic-depressive and was in and out of treatment throughout his life. As the years went by, he developed his talent in photography and derived great satisfaction as well as a modest income from his work. This was one area where he and his father could and did communicate, as Fred himself painted occasionally and the world of the arts was of interest to them both. When he was on leave from the army, where he served in the Medical Corps, and in the ensuing years, Freddy and my mother talked for hours during the day when Fred was at work; they were deeply fond of each other.

Roger was different from his troubled older brother. With his dark good looks and flirtatious way with girls, he was always out somewhere and always looking for the job of his dreams. He spoke with a pronounced stutter. As an adult, he worked at various small firms in the general field of technology and innovation. His talent for that kind of thinking was real, and he had several ideas for inventions that never seemed to come to anything but were always intriguing. He was a consummate charmer of a liar; the line between truth and fiction was never clear with him, nor did he seem to care. He fascinated and scared me, not unlike a cobra that is always watching, preparing to pounce. One night he did make his move, and I woke around 4:00 a.m. to find him sitting on my bed, watching me. He did not touch me, but the sense of intrusion was terrifying; I never slept with an unlocked door after that episode when he was around. During my sophomore year in high school, Roger became my tutor in plane geometry, a subject in which the highest grade I ever earned was a D. Roger tried hard to teach me the rudiments, but the combination of the math, my feelings about Roger, and a dour, unsympathetic teacher, Mr. Withers, made the course the biggest trial of my life at that time.

My mother tried hard to make us all into a family and included "the boys" in our lives, with sporadic and modest success. Their father did not seem to want them at home with him, although there was a bedroom for them in our apartment. I, of course, never mentioned my nighttime encounter, since it was all part of the secrecy that governed our lives, but I had little interest in having Roger around. Freddy and I had some good times in long conversations, listening to music, or playing double solitaire. Sometimes the two boys, both avid aficionados of jazz, would play trumpet (Roger) and trombone (Freddy), usually "Ciribiribin," which seemed to be the only piece they both knew well enough to practice.

Often, in the late afternoon before my parents' ritual of cocktails before dinner, Mother and I would shower in our separate bathrooms and then open the door between our bedrooms and talk while dressing for the evening. (We did not "dress" for dinner, but often showered and changed clothes at the end of the day.) We were unselfconscious, and frequently walked between the rooms toweling our hair or "making a point" by jabbing hairbrushes in the air. Both rooms had several windows without shades, which filled them with sun, air, and light, as well as offering a view of the apartment building across the street and Washington Square Park. I never gave a thought to the view that the tenants across the street had. It had not occurred to me that people actually looked into other people's apartments, until one afternoon when our house phone buzzed and there was Louis, the ever-present doorman, with a message: "The gentleman at the window on the sixth floor of the building across the street requests that the ladies in 6E please put on their clothes." Mother and I were stunned for a minute and then, still in the nude, looked out the window. There he was! A swarthy, round man, also undressed except for a yarmulke, stood staring at us. We retreated since he was creepy, to say the least, and for years relived Louis's comment, "Would the ladies in 6E please put on their clothes." It became part of the family lore, and looking back on the incident, it is a wonder that we did not question the actions of the man in the yarmulke, or Louis. Nor did we buy window shades, but we did modify our own behavior to the extent that we wrapped ourselves in bath towels as we strolled in and out of each other's room.

The ritual of the dinner hour, as well as the meal itself, was the focal point of our family life. It was the only time of day that we were all together, and everyone who was in residence at the time was expected to show up promptly. That took a bit of planning, as our usual dinnertime was sometime between 8:00 and 10:00 p.m., without much advance notice as to the exact hour. Many were the nights that I finished my homework and was more than hungry by the time dinner was ready. Mother became a creative and very good cook, making the plain wartime food appealing with advice from Fred about herbs, both fresh and dried. I learned about flavors and preparation of all kinds of meat and vegetables. We never had dessert, but had ample helpings of veal, beef, fish, chicken, squash, green beans, baked potatoes, and green salad, with her signature French dressing made with plenty of garlic, red wine vinegar, and a dash of dry mustard. I was not expected to do dishes, as dinner was late and we lingered over the meal for more than an hour, eating and talking, and by the end, I was half asleep.

My parents became quite expert in growing herbs of all kinds. Fred designed a label, Anderson Farm, and began to sell his dried herbs to hospitals and nursing homes as welcome additions to a salt-free diet. Over the years, it grew into a lively small business that he managed from the old garage at The Farm, where he processed the basil, thyme, winter savory, tarragon, and rosemary. He added herb-flavored vinegars to this repertoire and then various kinds of herbal mustards. Good, interesting food, with the addition of good wine after he retired, and liberal amounts of good talk became the hallmarks of life at The Farm.

There were two or three Christmas celebrations when Roger and Freddy were with us, and we felt like a family. On those Christmas Eves, Fred would come home early, laden with piles of packages that he would put in the living room, then he would pour a drink, light a cigarette, and survey the Christmas tree, which was in the corner of the dining room, bare and ready for decorating. We would all hang ornaments while Christmas music played on the record player, and there was much jocularity about who would put the star on the top. It was always Freddy or Roger, as they were both tall and really pleased to be asked. After the colored lights and shiny balls were in place, we would all take turns loading on the shiny tinsel, some in strands that we wound around the branches and some as "rain," thin pieces of tinfoil that shimmered whenever anyone walked by and caused the slightest breeze. Then we would place our presents to each other under the tree, with my mother having the largest pile, all boxes from Peck and Peck which Fred had brought home earlier that day. The last part of the ritual was a few moments of singing carols together while my mother accompanied us on the piano. It was extraordinary because we never sang at any other time of the year, separately or together, and so far as I knew, my mother never played the piano at any other time. While I enjoyed our being together and belting out the traditional music I loved, it felt unreal and not quite authentic. Then we had dinner together, and I hung my red flannel stocking on the mantle before going to bed. I was the only person in the family with a stocking and I opened it on Christmas morning by myself, since Mother and Fred slept until noon, as did Freddy and Roger. It was always full of small and useful things: hand lotion, mittens, pens, colored pencils, and, as I got older, barrettes, headbands, and socks. Sometimes there would be a special treasure, usually a miniature creature of some kind. I collected small animals and figures, first for a dollhouse and then to create small worlds of forests, villages, and lakes on small and large mirrors with tiny people skating. There was always a huge orange in the toe; it tasted very good, as breakfast was a non-meal in our life as a family, even on holidays.

Christmas Day was not nearly as memorable to me as Christmas Eve, but I reveled in all the presents and cheerful talk. I loved opening presents, and I received a number of gifts: sweaters and jackets, subscriptions to *Seventeen* magazine, records ("I'll Walk Alone" and "Whispering" being two favorites), books, stationery, and during college years, some simple and elegant pearl (costume jewelry, not real) necklaces and bracelets. Both my parents and my stepbrothers were appreciative of the gifts I gave them, many of them handmade. One year I made Fred a footstool in woodworking class at school, taught by Mr. Lonergan, who we later learned was a real Communist! Fred was truly touched and pleased by my work and the footstool, which he kept for many years in his workshop in the garage in that was part of The Farm,. I remain amazed to this day that I created the footstool, and that it never, as far as I know, collapsed or even teetered.

Despite the wartime gas rationing, my parents and I went to Bucks County, Pennsylvania, every weekend. If we could not buy gas for the car we took the train, but when we had enough of the little green paper squares in our ration books, Mother, Fred, and I would get into the old wooden station wagon with no heat and wooden seats. With Fred driving, we would go through the Holland Tunnel, onto the Pulaski Skyway, through the rancid, smelly Jersey Flats and turn onto Route 22, which took us through ever-diminishing traffic to

Frenchtown, New Jersey. There, we slowly crossed the languid Delaware River, landing in the lush green and sparsely populated Bucks County area of southeastern Pennsylvania. Another twenty-five minutes of driving down the winding, shady River Road next to the old canal and we would be in Tinicum, passing Old Man Haney's general store, and bouncing along a rutted red-dirt road for a couple of miles until we reached The Farm.

Fred had bought The Farm in 1936, for $3,000 cash, a story he was fond of telling. It was made up of 160 acres of fields, sixty of which were under cultivation, and a stunning fieldstone house built in 1803 with no running water, electricity, or heat. There, my parents slept late, raised herbs and lived a weekend life of hard work with plenty to drink at the end of each day. I split logs, carried water, weeded, mowed lawns by hand, and, since the house was quiet until noon on a regular basis, found a world in the many books that were on shelves and tables throughout the house. After a trip to the dreaded privy where wasps buzzed in the stink, my mornings were spent rolled up in a quilt on my bed. There I read all the Tom Swift books, Theodore Dreiser's *An American Tragedy,* the Nancy Drew books, old *LIFE* magazines dating back to 1936, O. Henry short stories, and the stories of Sherlock Holmes, whose precise reasoning and perceptive insights enthralled me. Over the ten to twelve years that I spent weekends and some weeks at The Farm, I found that there were always more books, and they were my companions through many lonely days.

My parents' marriage was a full-time preoccupation for my mother on the weekends, and I learned early on to make myself scarce and to keep my resentment at the loneliness and hard work of our weekend lives under control. We had no telephone, few friends in Bucks County and seldom invited friends from New York to join us. Our life at The Farm was essentially isolated. During the evenings, Fred drank blended whiskey and usually fell asleep with his head on or near his dinner plate. My mother also drank whiskey in the evenings, but I do not recall ever seeing her drunk. She and I cleared the table and did the dishes by the light of a kerosene lamp, heating the hot water on the large woodstove known as "Big Bridey," and then I went to bed. She must have gotten him up the steep, winding stairs to the second floor somehow, but I never saw that effort, as they stayed up late well into the early morning hours. I often heard the low murmur of their voices when I would wake up in the night, which was quietly reassuring. It was understood that his drinking was not to be discussed, along with other subjects I was expressly told not to talk about in front of him: sex, the bathroom, and religion. Fortunately, politics was very much a topic for talk—interesting talk. I learned that my stepfather was an immensely intelligent, widely read person who enjoyed extended conversation about ideas and taught me to appreciate the beauty of the thoughtful exchange of knowledge, opinion, and clear questions. More than once, when I would say I knew I had an idea but could not find the way to express it, he said that until stated, the idea does not exist. I had some private doubts about that principle as I grew up, but it was a standard that served me well during my high school and college years, and I believe I acquired an ability to say what I meant.

On Sunday afternoon, usually around 4:00 p.m., we would load the car with buckets of fresh flowers, packages of herbs, unfinished books, and heavy sweaters and jackets. When that effort was completed, I clambered into the backseat, my stepfather took the wheel, and with my mother next to him, we would set forth for the City. Time was of the essence, as we all wanted to be back in time to hear Jack Benny's radio show at 7:00 p.m. and Fred Allen at 8:00, with Senator Claghorn being our favorite character on the show.

From time to time, I met people who expressed sympathy and even concern for me and the life I led with my very particular parents. As I have matured, I certainly understand why they would have felt that way. While I felt unfailingly and consistently loved by my mother, I often felt unsafe; I distrusted and was intimidated by my stepfather, and sometimes was neglected by both. Those feelings were intensified when my beloved Hazel explained to me that she would not work in the same house with "that man" and left my life. I was stunned, but old enough at eight or nine to look after myself, which I did most of the time. In later years, I came to appreciate Fred for his deep intelligence and breadth of knowledge, as well as his appreciation of many kinds of music, his intellectual curiosity about a range of topics, including history and politics, and his clarity of thought. He had an extraordinary gift for conversation. He showed me that he cared about me by writing thoughtful, long letters on yellow legal paper, encouraging me when I was doubtful, praising me when I did well, and letting me know he was truly pleased and respectful of the choices I was making. He did not ever criticize or correct me explicitly, but had a way of asking questions with a gentleness that surprised me and made me pay attention.

CHAPTER V

URBAN TEEN

Becoming seventh graders at Friends Seminary on 15th Street and Stuyvesant Square meant that my friend Clare and I were liberated from the school bus and could walk to school, or take the 14th Street cross-town bus if we wanted to spend a dime of our allowance. With our book bags dangling from our shoulders and our saddle shoes (preferably gray with dirt), knee socks complementing our sweaters (buttoned up the back), and pleated skirts, we were unremarkable members of the large number of children growing up in New York City in the Forties. On days when we had any extra money (from babysitting, usually), we would prowl the aisles of S. Klein or pop in and out of the hundreds of small shops along 14th Street in hopes of finding items of fashion that we could afford. One day I found some black ballet slippers for three dollars, which I wore delightedly for a few weeks until the day I was caught in the rain and the paper lining disintegrated into a smelly, soggy mass. One of our frequent stops on the way home in the late afternoon was a pause at The Fat Man's Store on Third Avenue and 10th Street, a unique emporium owned by Clare's parents. I was simply stunned at the size of the blue boxer shorts and gray pajamas which were displayed on the walls. They were measured in feet, not inches. Dr. and Mrs. Greenberger (he had been a dentist before working in the family business) were slight in stature and large in presence. Watching them working with their clientele from all walks of life, including the circus, was a lesson in meeting the needs of people who were "different" in a respectful, professional way. We usually collected a cookie, Clare got a hug, and I received a hurried smile, and with that we were off to our respective homes; first to 10th Street and Fifth Avenue where Clare lived, and then to Washington Square where I lived with my mother and stepfather. One of my rituals was to stop and talk with the shopkeepers on 8th Street if I went that way, or with the doorman at 29 Washington Square if I walked in that direction. Some days I cut through the park, which was full of children playing, men of all generations hunched over the cement checkerboards that lined the MacDougal Street side, and of course, many dogs; some on leashes and some not, but all made for hazardous walking as I picked my way among their piles of droppings.

Although I definitely was not a prankster, nor did I ever challenge the rules and expectations, I had one experience in the seventh grade that was outside of any school experiences I had ever had. *Forever Amber*, a best seller of the time, was considered to be a naughty book. I don't think anyone ever said it was, but we seventh grade girls found it positively exciting and almost unbelievable. There was one chapter in which Amber has her clothes removed by one of her swains, and they become entangled on a bed or couch in an episode that takes up about three pages. The descriptions of the panting and groaning were tame by today's standards, but for us the book was daring and completely engrossing. We took turns passing it around, wrapping it carefully in brown paper. My turn to take the book home came on the last day before spring vacation started. I received the tainted goods in the girls' locker room and could not wait to read it, so I went into a toilet stall, locked the door, and gave myself up to the transporting moment. I was there for a long time; long enough that everyone, including the janitor, left for vacation, locking the doors and turning out all the lights in the halls. Realizing that I was the only person in the building, and having no idea when anyone would return since vacation had started, I peered into the dark hallway outside the locker room and was scared stiff as it was too dark; and besides, the doors to the outside would be locked. After some thought, I realized there was a small window high up in the locker room. It was my only hope. So, I deposited the naughty book—which seemed really silly by then—in the bottom of the trash can, covered it with the used paper towels, and dragged an old chair over to the wall. I climbed up and found the window was unlocked. After tossing my gym clothes out, which were due for a trip to the laundry during vacation, followed by my books, I scrambled up, squeezing out and trying to close the frosted glass once I was safely outside. I did not linger and started the long walk from 15th Street and Third Avenue to Washington Square feeling partly pleased with myself for getting out and partly foolish to have gotten locked in at all. I knew I could not confess why I was late getting home and offered the excuse that I had been reading in the library and had lost track of time.

My initiation into the titillation of being ogled by boys happened when I was fourteen. I began to be aware of a gang of boys whistling at me as I crossed Waverly Place and entered the park on a fall afternoon after school. Soon they added a chorus of "Hiya, Red, how's your dog?" This was referring to my then reddish hair and to my black cocker spaniel, Cappy, which told me they had been watching me over some time period. I knew that "nice girls" did not pay attention to such uncouth youths, so I walked on, displaying what I hoped was an aloof disdain on one hand, while feeling ever so grown-up and vaguely seductive on the other. Perhaps modeling myself after Lauren Bacall in *To Have and Have Not* was paying off! This activity became a standard part of my day for several weeks, with no effort on their part to speak to me and certainly not I to them. Then the moment came when the leader of the group, a tall, dangerously handsome West Indian boy who was seventeen or so, stopped me and politely introduced himself, "Hello, I'm Nat." I was flustered, and before I remembered what not to say, I blurted out, "I'm Edes." Nat's response was, "Who?" I gave my name again. As my flushed, sweating self gathered a modicum of poise, I responded with "Alright" when he asked if he could walk with me. We both knew, instinctively, that he could not take me to my apartment building where Louis, the pompous, angular doorman, monitored all comings and goings. So, we parted on the corner of MacDougal and Washington Place, he to return to the group of young men and me to my apartment, praying that my mother had not seen me from her chair by the window overlooking the Park, her usual place in the afternoon.

A couple of evenings later, Nat called me at home and my sweating started again. Phone calls were not usual events and, when they did occur, were usually Clare or another one of my school friends. I had a fast, silent conversation with myself while agreeing to meet him at 9:00 p.m. under the street lamp on MacDougal and Waverly Place when I took Cappy out for his evening walk. Lying to my mother either explicitly or implicitly was something I had seldom done, and when I did, it was about such things as whether I had finished the revolting lima beans at dinner or had completed a household chore. I was and am a poor liar. Nonetheless, though I knew it was a dangerous decision, I snapped on Cappy's leash, checked my Windsor Pink Revlon lipstick, and sallied forth into night. Nat appeared immediately, and we walked around the park (I was forbidden to go inside the park after dark) for half an hour or so, when predictably he reached for my shoulders and kissed me. It was a thrilling, awful, squishy experience, and he stared at me, no doubt calculating his next move. In a burst of good sense, I said good night and Cappy and I fled for the safety of Louis's presence. As I entered our apartment, my mother looked at me with a piercing gaze which made me feel less than honest. I gave her my usual good-night kiss with no words exchanged and went to my room to go to bed. When I got home from school the next day, I found a note pinned to my pillow with a copy of a newspaper article about Nat, who had been arrested twice for engaging in Peeping Tom behavior. My mother's words were, "I thought you would like to know." True to our relationship and the times, we did not discuss the matter until years later. I did not meet Nat again and lived in fear that I would see him on the street, as I had no idea how I would manage such an encounter. I spent the next three years walking home without cutting through the park.

As a teenager growing up in Manhattan during the Forties, my friends and I experienced a degree of independence from an early age that is almost unimaginable now. Without cell phones for checking in and being checked on, my friends and I visited a wide variety of places and people. Our range of interests was eclectic, to say the least. One Saturday when I was fourteen or so, my friend, Mary Burdell, and I went to see a matinee of *The Barber of Seville* at the old Metropolitan Opera House; where we stood for the three acts, having paid $3.00 for the privilege of standing and leaning on the well-worn velvet covered barricade between the seats and the standing room area. Leaving there, we proceeded to Broadway where we joined a long line of patient teenagers waiting to see Frank Sinatra go into one of the theatres where he was performing. Mary was besotted with "Frankie." I did not share her enthusiasm for him, but I loved being part of the scene in Times Square on a coldish winter evening with all the colored lights blazing and the taxis honking. After catching a glimpse of her idol, we dove into the underground of the City and took our respective subways home, she to Gramercy Park and I to Washington Square. Other weekend activities included an occasional movie when we had saved enough allowance money, the Metropolitan Museum, which we rode to on a Fifth Avenue bus with an open top for a nickel, going to Hamburger Heaven or Schraffts' with a parent or visiting relative, and one of our favorites, going to the Automat of 42nd Street. I never tired of putting 25¢ in the slot and watching the tray inside the small glass window slowly turn producing a sandwich, always made with soft white bread, or a piece of apple pie with a heavy crust, which was extracted carefully after opening the little glass door. Sitting at a table in the Automat offered a view of the population of New York City that was endlessly interesting—the "bums," as they were called, sitting near the businessmen (few women) in coats and ties headed for Grand Central Station and their train home or to the offices around the City, having just arrived. Everyone of all ages and backgrounds seemed to go to the Automat, and it was a busy place day and night.

My best friend, Clare, and I walked to school together everyday. Often, we would be joined by some fellow students who lived on 11th and 12th Streets, and we would move as a unit up Fifth Avenue and across 14th Street, arriving at Third Avenue, which was the edge of The Bowery. (On rainy days we took the 14th Street cross-town bus for 10¢.) We stepped over the men, and a few women, who were lying on the sidewalk or leaning against the buildings, with liquor bottles scattered about and the stench of unwashed people who soiled themselves permeating the air. We did not fear them, though we were uncomfortable at the sights and were always glad to get to 15th Street where Friends Seminary stood, as it has since 1786. The Quaker Meeting House and the school were places of safety and the center of our social as well as academic lives during the war years and after. A basic tenet of our Quaker education was concern for issues of social justice. Experiencing the laboratory of The Bowery was an integral part of that education. One of my activities in high school was participating in the Current Events Club, which was a kind of debating group. We traveled throughout the five boroughs to public and independent schools discussing issues of inequity in our society and the ideals of the United Nations, to which we were deeply committed. The Quaker commitment to peace was central to my life, as an individual as well as an American citizen, and I spoke about it with youthful passion on numerous occasions.

Issues of social inequity affected my classmates' and my choices for activities outside of school as well, with one vivid example being a summer experience in Tivoli as a strawberry picker for the State of New York. It was a program designed to offer summer employment for teenagers and to provide the farmers with low-cost labor, as minimum wage for teenagers was not part of the picture in 1946. In July, between our freshman and sophomore years, four of us signed up to be part of a cadre of seventy girls, chiefly from the Bronx, East Harlem, Harlem, Washington Heights, and Brooklyn, and mainly Black or Hispanic. We were the only private school girls and among the very few Whites. We took the train along the scenic Hudson River to Tivoli, where we were met by a blue dump truck.

The young man who was the driver and greeter was monosyllabic as he tossed our suitcases (only one each) into the back and jerked his head to indicate that we were to ride in the back along with the bags. As we climbed onto the back of the truck and sat on the floor—which was full of bits of dirt, grass, and unnamed substances that were mainly sticky—we were silent. We were dropped off at one of two large barn-like buildings in which thirty-five girls stayed in dormitory style on the second floor, with a bathroom (one toilet, two sinks, and one shower) at each end and two lines of iron bunk beds against opposite walls. There were four windows, two at each end, and one staircase to the ground floor. Meals were presented cafeteria-style in another large barn-like structure down the road.

In the mornings, we were awakened at 5:00 a.m. and had an hour to make our beds, dress, wash, and get to the cafeteria, where we had cold cereal and juice and made our lunches from rows of bologna, Wonder Bread, peanut butter, jelly, and mayonnaise. By 6:00 a.m., with brown paper bags in hand, we were loaded onto trucks and driven to the various strawberry fields in the cool, dampish early morning air. By 7:00 a.m., we were in our assigned rows, with instructions to "put the green and rotten ones on the bottom of the basket and the pretty ones on top." At 11:00 a.m., we stopped and took our baskets to be checked and weighed. At 7¢ a quart, we watched very carefully as the results of our labors were examined. Each day an announcement was made of who had picked the most, and Christie Rinehart, one of "The Friends Four," consistently won the applause. Her biggest day was eighty-seven quarts, which was a lot of berries! We had one hour for lunch, and were given water to wash down the Wonder Bread sandwiches and shown where the toilet or outhouse facilities were. Then it was back to the fields at 1:00 p.m. The day finished at 4:00 p.m. with another round of weighing and examining. We got back onto the trucks and were taken to our dormitories, where the lines for the shower were daunting. After supper at 6:00 p.m., we drifted around, and on Saturdays we went to a weekly sing-along event. Otherwise, we read and wrote letters home from our bunks. Lights were out at 9:00 p.m. As soon as the matron had turned out the three bare bulbs dangling from the ceiling, several of the girls would go to the windows and begin a keening sound, calling for the one man we all had met when we arrived. He did not show up, though once he walked by, causing the keening to turn into shrill squeals.

While we from Friends Seminary did not mix very successfully as a group, one of us from "The Friends Four" as we dubbed ourselves, was elected by the group every Sunday to be the "proctor" or chief "student supervisor" for the week. At the end of the month, the strawberry season was over and green beans were ready to pick. Many of us were invited to continue, and while I felt good about being asked to stay—the farmers made the decisions and I had worked hard to do a good job—I decided to go home, knowing that I had not signed up for green beans and could make more money babysitting. I did not like the job or the surroundings, although I felt good about making and fulfilling the commitment. When three members of our group left, Fred wrote me some thoughtful letters telling me how proud he was of the job I was doing. When I decided not to re-enroll for green beans, he told me when I got home that I had made a good decision and, again, that he was proud of me. Spoken compliments were rare in our house, and I treasure his words to this day.

Like most teenagers—urban, suburban, or rural—our social lives were fraught with peer peril. We obsessed over questions like: "Does he like me?" "Who asked you to the dance?" "Do I look freaky in that tunic and bloomers (gym uniform)?" "Will he come to watch me play basketball? I hope he does/doesn't." "What is your curfew?" "Isn't he cute?" "Did you see his sweaty palms last night? They made a stain on my dress." We were always looking for a place to have a party where the parents were not home, and occasionally we were successful. While there was some drinking, it was the game of Spin the Bottle that was our main entertainment in eighth and ninth grades. As New York apartments were small, the most inviting places to play the game were in the coat closets. The smell of wet wool, the black galoshes underfoot, and the lack of air made the experience of being "chosen" by the bottle as it spun around truly unpleasant, even as we professed to like it. The various gropings, pantings, and wetness on our faces left us wanting to wash and unable to look at the person with whom we had just groped and panted. These gatherings were usually on Saturday night, and Monday morning at school brought an agony of self-consciousness, wondering what the boys thought of us. It did not occur to us girls that the boys might be feeling the same way.

By the time I was sixteen, I had a real boyfriend who was a senior and treated me with respect and courtesy to a degree that I had not experienced in my male classmates. Jerry was a bit taller than me, with fair skin, freckles, very blue eyes, and closely cut curly black hair. He was one of the better-dressed boys, and his tweed jackets and neatly knotted ties were much admired. He was smart, thoughtful, and quiet. He and I were an "item," and he took me to Eddie Condon's in the Village, where we drank rye and ginger ale, smoked, laughed, and held hands while the jazz musicians played. It was a glorious evening, and I remember the green plaid taffeta dress I wore. I felt pretty and grown-up. This was a real date, and it was all I had imagined that it would be. Jerry took me home, and I floated into the apartment, wreathed in smiles I am sure. My mother emerged from their bedroom, gave me a huge hug, and we all went to bed. Jerry and I maintained our relationship until he went off to Tufts, at which point we both moved on to lives in other places with other people.

CHAPTER VI

FROM GOOD TO GLAMOUR

In 1947, when I was fifteen, there was a major blizzard that became an event to remember about post-World War II New York City. Walking up and down Fifth Avenue on top of the blanket of crystalline snow was exhilarating. The City was silent, with buses and cars unable to move. The absence of any sound but the crackling as we stepped onto the snowy, sparkling crust made walking in the middle of Fifth Avenue an adventure that we celebrated with singing, sticking out our tongues to catch the flakes, and shrieking as we made snow angels on the corner of 14th Street. Somehow, the freedom of that moment became a metaphor for the release from fear and the sense of renewal in our country. The death of President Franklin Roosevelt in 1945 and the arrival of Harry Truman as president had sent deep shock waves of emotion through my parents' community of friends and colleagues. When the news was announced on the radio, my mother cried as she was brushing her hair and changing her clothes for dinner. I seldom saw her weep and never had seen her sob with great noisy gulps. I felt her sense of uncertainty and unease with what would happen without the person who had led us through the Depression and the war. In the months that followed, she and Fred expressed support and respect for President Truman, particularly about the GI Bill and the Marshall Plan, but they never seemed to feel the sense of connection with him as they had with President Roosevelt.

As the end of high school in June 1949 began to loom in our lives and our workload at school increased, the prospect of college applications and entrance exams entered the conversation among us, the students, and with our teachers. The most important person in our lives was Earle Hunter, the brilliant, quixotic, and devoted head of the upper school at Friends Seminary, who was also our history teacher and the college counselor. He was a strong, slight man, with a shock of thick gray hair that he brushed back, often running his fingers through it. He always wore a vest buttoned neatly over his trim midsection. All students took his Modern European History course as juniors and the challenging American History that defined senior year. The workload was heavy and excuses for nonperformance unthinkable. The classes were full of discussion of issues, past and present. His point of view was always from the perspective of the effects of events on people and the striving for equity of opportunity. His expectations for each of us were consistently high, and earning an A from him was an accomplishment held almost in awe by classmates. We felt his dedication to us and our progress. He had a gravelly voice and an original style of teaching that included information liberally laced with wry humor. One gray February day, I was fumbling for a response in history class and he prodded me by saying, with a twinkle in his piercing blue eyes, "Powell, use your head for something besides a hat rack!" And I did. My classmates and I loved being singled out for the "hat rack" admonition. Also, I knew him from another perspective, as I became the babysitter for his young son, the first child from his second marriage to a former student. I saw him as a devoted father with a rather puckish sense of humor, whose face lit up when he held his toddler in his arms. I understood that none of the more personal aspects of my babysitting for his family was to enter the student-teacher relationship, and they did not. His interest in me and my progress as a person and a student was a central support and motivation for me, offering a strong male presence that I trusted and never let me down. The time at school was the center of my life during these years, with Dr. Hunter being the most important person, whose opinion mattered and whose praise I valued. My decision to become a teacher, and the kind of teacher I have tried to be, were influenced greatly by him.

During the fall of senior year, college became the sole topic of conversation and focus of attention. Dr. Hunter insisted on our applying to four or five colleges, keeping our expectations in check. I wanted Vassar or Smith and wasn't sure which was first—backups were Carleton and Bennington. One cold, gray December day, I took the train to Poughkeepsie to see Vassar and had a daunting interview with the venerable and venerated Dean Mildred Thompson in a Victorian parlor full of scarlet velvet draperies and unyielding stuffed chairs. As I waited for her, it occurred to me that my snowy boots were dripping onto the thick Oriental carpet. By the time Dean Thompson came in, I was trying to hide my feet under the sofa where I was perched uneasily. I felt clumsy as I leapt to my dripping feet. She was gracious and put me at ease, seemingly not noticing my oozing boots. As this was my mother's alma mater, I was aware that being accepted was especially important.

After what seemed like an interminable winter, spring came, and with the warm weather, came the letters of acceptance and rejection. The moment of truth, when *the* letters would come, was on a Saturday for the bigger colleges, including the Seven Sisters. I had applied to two Sisters, Vassar and Smith, because both offered teacher training as part of a major, and I knew I wanted to teach the elementary grades. There was no way I was leaving the City when my parents piled into the elderly Ford station wagon and headed to The Farm for a weekend in April. I stayed in the apartment, watching for the mail on Saturday morning and planning to take the bus to New Jersey, where my mother would meet me that afternoon. The mail arrived and I had two thick letters, which I knew meant good news. Having already been accepted at Carleton and Bennington, I was absolutely euphoric and could not wait to tell my parents or my classmates and Dr. Hunter on Monday. That afternoon I boarded the bus for Frenchtown, New Jersey, at 34th Street, with the knowledge that my parents were going to be thrilled for me—and they were. The bus dropped me at the footbridge across the Delaware River, where I could see the station wagon waiting on the other side. I galloped across waving both letters, shouting, "I'm in! I'm in!" My mother was beaming and could not stop smiling as we drove down River Road to The Farm. My waiting stepfather took one look at my mother and me, and his face broke into a huge smile as we got out of the car. He gave me an enormous hug. Both parents toasted me and my future college career when the ever-present pre-dinner drinks were poured. Both made it clear that whichever I chose, Smith or Vassar, would be fine. After some consideration, I chose Vassar because I would graduate with New York State certification as a teacher for grades K–6. The assumption that I would have a career was part of the context of our family life, and teaching was what I had been drawn to from the time I "taught" Evelyn to read. Also, it was one of the few options available to women. When I was fourteen, I had flirted with the notion of being a trial lawyer, but it lasted only a few weeks, and then I went back to my lifelong dream of being a teacher of young children. My mother advised me never to learn to type, because if I did "I might have to," and her view of my future did not include being anyone's secretary. Several of my friends attended the Katherine Gibbs Secretarial School after graduating from college, but I began my teaching career as an assistant teacher in the four-year-old class at the Child Education Foundation.

Being a senior in high school was heady business indeed. There were the responsibilities that were inherent in being the school leaders and examples of exemplary behavior to younger students. There were various privileges, such as choosing an elective course for the spring term and choosing a graduation speaker—Norman Thomas, head of the Socialist Party, a decision that benefited from the deft guidance of Dr. Hunter. More interesting to us girls were the numerous conversations about long white graduation dresses. (Lace was very "in" during 1949, and my dress was perfect, with a sleeveless lace bodice and a long tulle skirt.) The most tantalizing discussions focused on the Graduation Party, which would happen after we went home with our parents following the 8:00 p.m. ceremony; when we would change our clothes and sally forth for an "all-nighter." We imagined all sorts of possibilities, mainly vague, and dependent on which boy did what and to whom. At the same time, we knew that sex was a major taboo. The worst that could happen to a girl in the Forties and Fifties was to get pregnant. Our parents, especially our mothers, made that clear. Sex was for marriage, period. However, attending the several parties added up to the much-anticipated whole night with no curfew, when much of our time was spent walking or taking subways from one part of the City to another. Following my mother's firm admonition to always accept the first boy who invited me, I went with Francis Valente, a nice boy with model manners whose father was a judge, which was noteworthy to me and my friends. However, his parents did not go along with "no curfew," and at 3:00 a.m. he departed the party given by a classmate on the roof of the Chelsea Hotel. I had no intention of going home since I had permission to stay out all night and waved him off without a backward glance. In a burst of self-confidence, I attached myself to an alumnus named Al Burlen who had appeared at the party. He was tall and blond, with an athletic build. I had admired him when he was a senior, and I a lowly sophomore. We wound up walking home at dawn from a party on 81st Street. The sun was coming up and Manhattan was bathed in a soft, rosy light that I had never seen before. There were six or seven of us, singing, sleepy, and animated as we made our way to Washington Square. When we arrived at the Arch, several went their separate ways, and Al walked me home across the park, dropping me at the front door of my building under the watchful eye of the all-knowing Louis. I was as content as I had ever been falling into bed and sleeping for nine solid hours. When I woke up in the early afternoon, I felt as though I had become a real adult.

Arriving at Vassar on a clear September afternoon in 1949, in the immortal Ford station wagon of the war years and after, we pulled up in front of Strong House, the dormitory to which I had been assigned. The campus was filled with girls and their families carrying lamps, pillows, and various pieces of furniture. I thought it the most exciting place I had ever been and went looking for my room and roommate. The first person I met was the memorable Dean Thompson, who, it turned out, was my advisor and the dormitory supervisor, aka "Matron." My room was on the second floor, and my parents and I lugged the obligatory trunk, bedspread, pillowcases, and new Royal typewriter, my graduation present, up the metal-rimmed steps covered in well-worn dark green linoleum. We arrived at room 205 to find that it was two rooms, with the other occupant already settled in. Carol Hoover was the daughter of a missionary family stationed in China. She had not been to the United States for nine years. Her goal in life was to go into the theatre as a lighting designer. She was awkward and earnest, a tall girl with a hopeful smile and long blond hair that was not coiffed in the style of the moment, a pageboy. She and I decided to share the small room as a bedroom and use the larger one as a sitting room, an arrangement that suited both of us. The communal bathroom was down the hall, with hooks for our bags of toiletries. Two shower stalls, multiple toilet stalls, and wash basins completed the facilities. There were a dozen or so girls on the hall, some from our class and some from upper classes. I found the older girls to be incredibly sophisticated and poised. Their page-boys always seemed sleek and perfectly turned under. Their gray or plaid Bermuda shorts never looked rumpled. Their knee socks stayed up as they were supposed to. Their cardigan sweaters, buttoned down the back and worn with blouses with Peter Pan collars, always seemed to fit perfectly, even those with ragged elbows which were a mark of genteel chic that I never achieved or understood. Within several weeks, I had met some classmates who were kindred spirits and with whom I shared a similar sense of humor as well as an attitude toward academics. We enjoyed our classes, were interested in doing well, and found the world of college to be a feast of opportunities which we had not imagined. I loved walking to classes in different buildings, carrying books and notebooks in my arms, as any kind of book bag was considered to be only for earnest and unstylish people.

I was excused from freshman English because I tested out (thank you, Friends Seminary) and was put into a course in classical English literature taught by Miss Giffin, a scholar whose teaching style was dry, but whose knowledge of Old English literature was vast. She recited *Beowulf* and *The Canterbury Tales* in the Old English of each period, which I found remarkable, although it was not a skill to which I aspired. The homework she assigned that included memorization was tedious, and I never developed a fondness for Chaucer, which was her favorite. The course in child study was fascinating, and I learned how to observe the behavior of young children as well as the stages of development, which would inform my teaching career in the future. In a tactic designed to avoid chemistry and physics, I elected geology, which turned out to be one of my better decisions as well as very demanding. It was one of the few classes that met on several Saturdays to accommodate the field trips to various locales along the Hudson River, where we studied rock formations and trilobites. Dr. Werthan was a dedicated teacher and scientist who instilled a respect for the power of nature's forces in us, almost in spite of ourselves; since I was not the only one who had thought it would be a "gut" course. One of the courses that made a lasting impression on me was political science with Mr. Musolf. For whatever reason, I behaved like a smarty-pants throughout the term. I knew it, but did not stop making wisecracks and calling attention to myself. I found the material to be engaging and the instruction demanding, but persisted in the behavior which I did not like in myself. The result was the one and only D that I received in my four years at Vassar. It was deserved and humiliating. Knowing that I had to tell my mother before my grades were sent home, I took the unusual action of calling her. That moment was one of the low points of my eighteen years, and I never had to make such a call again. I have no recollection of how she responded, but I am sure she must have been calm, knowing that I was already chastising myself.

The academic life at Vassar was central to our lives, but was not the only engrossing aspect of campus life. Two girls in particular, Joan Rapp and Peggy Loizeaux, who we called "Bird," became my good friends. Joan and I both worked at the college bookstore to earn our spending money. Bird spent every possible moment at the theatre, working with a much-respected drama teacher named Hallie Flanagan. When we had the money and the time, we often walked to the movie house on the corner of Raymond Avenue and sat in the back with our feet up on the seats in front of us, munching popcorn and being noisy. We liked to play bridge and did so occasionally when we could put a game together. We had little expertise, but we smoked and dealt our cards with a great deal of good-natured joshing and no particular competition. Our favorite activity together was something we called "one o'clocks," when we stayed up until 2:00 a.m. or later discussing life, politics, and the pursuit of men, preferably those attending Yale. Joan was the belle of our trio and knew a series of Yalies who came to call on Wednesdays (Hump Night, so called because it marked the middle of the week) and Saturdays. She sometimes stayed out late, past curfew, which was 10:00 p.m. on Wednesdays and 11:00 p.m. on Saturdays. (We all broke this rule at some time in our four years at college.) She would whistle or throw pebbles at my window, and I would unlock the big window on the fire escape, hoping that the elderly patrolman with the huge flashlight, who made hourly rounds of the dormitory, would not appear. Joan was tall and willowy, with a lovely singing voice, and was recruited to sing in the group known as The Night Owls, which Bird and I found very impressive. I sang in the chapel choir and became slightly involved with one of the campus newspapers, but did not pursue either for very long. Between homework, friends, student teaching, and working at accounting twenty hours a week at the bookstore, I did not have much interest in or time for other activities. I spent any extra time in long, endless conversations about the meaning of life, boys, sex, and politics with people from other classes as well as my own. My friends were eclectic and interesting. After college, most of us became wives and mothers in keeping with the times, and many of us pursued careers in a wide range of not-for-profit and for-profit fields. My eyes were opened to various ways of life that I had never heard of. For instance, I had never known anyone who "made a debut" or "came out," and found myself invited to a number of elegant balls and cotillions during the Thanksgiving and Christmas vacations of my freshman and sophomore years. Acquiring suitable evening dresses was a full-time occupation, and one which my mother became immersed in with me when I went home for my one fall weekend away from campus and we went shopping. I danced many nights away in New York and Boston, where the parties were numerous and exciting. I felt glamorous and sophisticated on the surface and unsure, but intrigued beneath. This aspect of New York society opened up all kinds of questions as well as possible aspirations which were part of my education during those years. Balancing the life of the affluent with the issues of equity that dominated my Quaker education and home life became a central concern of my freshman and sophomore years at Vassar, and influenced many of my life decisions in later years.

Although it was clear to me as a girl growing up in this post World War II era that getting my "MRS" was the most important degree I could earn, life in my family put a high premium on achievement and education. In addition, my mother believed passionately that every woman should be sure that she have some money of her own, no matter how small an amount, to spend in any way she chose without having to account to a husband or anyone. Not surprisingly given her life's experiences, she also believed that I must be able to support my family should it become necessary as it had for her as well as for my grandmother.

When I graduated from Vassar my parents told me I had three months to find a job to be able to support myself and I would have to pay rent to live at home. Not being stupid, I figured I would rather pay rent to a landlord and be independent which I'm sure was my parents' plan. So, I found my first teaching job at the Child Education Foundation on East 81st Street and moved into a one-room apartment next to the Third Avenue El with Patsy Pulling, a friend from college.

And so, armed with a healthy sense of myself, an excellent education, and boundless optimism, I launched myself into the future.

Cast of Characters

PARENTS

	Helen Ann Ranney Powell	b. 1906 – d. 1960
	Talcott Williams Powell	b. 1900 – d. 1937
(stepfather)	Frederick Otwell Anderson	b. 1903 – d. 1986

BROTHERS

(half)	David Talcott Powell	b. 1924 – d. 1945
(step)	Frederick Alden Anderson	b. 1924 – d. 1988
	Roger DeGourley Anderson	b. 1925 –

GRANDPARENTS

(maternal)	William St. John Ranney	N/A
	Susan Fisher Bradshaw Ranney	b. 1881 – d. 1976
(paternal)	Lyman Pierson Powell	b. 1866 – d. 1946
	Gertrude Wilson Powell	b. 1876(?) – d. 1950

OTHER PEOPLE WHO MATTERED

Caretaker and housekeeper	Hazel
Best friend/"almost sister"	Susan Hunter
Susan's mother and my godmother	Isobel Strong Hunter
History teacher and mentor	Earl Hunter
Best friend in school	Clare Greenberger

8625372R0

Made in the USA
Lexington, KY
16 February 2011